Dear Parent:
Your child's love of reading starts here!

Every child learns to read in a different way and at his or her own speed. Some go back and forth between reading levels and read favorite books again and again. Others read through each level in order. You can help your young reader improve and become more confident by encouraging his or her own interests and abilities. From books your child reads with you to the first books he or she reads alone, there are I Can Read Books for every stage of reading:

SHARED READING
Basic language, word repetition, and whimsical illustrations, ideal for sharing with your emergent reader

BEGINNING READING
Short sentences, familiar words, and simple concepts for children eager to read on their own

READING WITH HELP
Engaging stories, longer sentences, and language play for developing readers

READING ALONE
Complex plots, challenging vocabulary, and high-interest topics for the independent reader

ADVANCED READING
Short paragraphs, chapters, and exciting themes for the perfect bridge to chapter books

I Can Read Books have introduced children to the joy of reading since 1957. Featuring award-winning authors and illustrators and a fabulous cast of beloved characters, I Can Read Books set the standard for beginning readers.

A lifetime of discovery begins with the magical words **"I Can Read!"**

Visit www.icanread.com for information
on enriching your child's reading experience.

I Can Read Book® is a trademark of HarperCollins Publishers.

Paddington's Day Off. Text copyright © 2017 by Michael Bond. Adapted from the original story written by Michael Bond.
Illustrations copyright © 2017 by HarperCollins Publishers. All rights reserved. Manufactured in U.S.A. No part of this book may be
used or reproduced in any manner whatsoever without written permission except in the case of brief quotations embodied in critical
articles and reviews. For information address HarperCollins Children's Books, a division of HarperCollins Publishers, 195 Broadway,
New York, NY 10007.
www.icanread.com

Library of Congress Control Number: 2016935905
ISBN 978-0-06-243074-8 (trade bdg.) — ISBN 978-0-06-243073-1 (pbk.)

17 18 19 20 21 LSCC 10 9 8 7 6 5 4 3 2 ❖ First Edition

I Can Read!

BEGINNING 1 READING

PADDINGTON'S
Day Off

Michael Bond
illustrated by R. W. Alley

HARPER
An Imprint of HarperCollinsPublishers

One day Paddington went
out for a walk.

He got out his basket on wheels
and put on his coat and hat.

He wanted to see his friend

Mr. Gruber, who owned a shop

in the Portobello Road market.

Mr. Gruber made them some cocoa.

Paddington had some buns to eat.

"It's such a beautiful day,"

Mr. Gruber said.

"Let's take the day off!"

Mr. Gruber closed up the shop.
Paddington hung a sign
on the door.

Paddington and Mr. Gruber

invited Jonathan and Judy

to come along, too.

They packed a lunch.

Paddington brought his suitcase,

a map, and his guidebook.

He also brought his opera glasses.

Mr. Gruber pointed out
lots of things as they passed
by stores and cafés.

Paddington stopped and said hello
to everyone they saw along the way.

Mr. Gruber led them
through a gate into a park.
Paddington was amazed.

There was so much to see and do!

They stopped for lunch by the lake.
Paddington dipped his paws
into the water while he ate
his marmalade sandwich.

At the amusement area,
they played on the slide
and the swings.

Then Mr. Gruber said,

"What's that sound?"

They all stopped to listen.

They heard music playing.

They walked farther into the park

and found a little bandstand.

A band was playing!

Mr. Gruber found some empty chairs.

They all sat down.

Mr. Gruber read the program.

"They are playing

a famous Surprise Symphony!"

Paddington loved surprises.

He wondered what

the surprise would be.

Paddington decided to ask
the band about the surprise.
He walked around the bandstand.
There was a door marked "Private."
It opened easily.

Inside, Paddington looked around.

It was dark and dusty and gloomy.

The door closed behind him.

Paddington pushed on the door.

It wouldn't open!

Paddington found an old broom.

He pounded on the ceiling.

Mr. Gruber wondered
where Paddington had gone.
The music was playing.
It didn't sound right.

Bump, bump, bump!
The sound was coming
from under the stage.

Bump, BUMP, BUMP!

The conductor jumped.

The sound was coming

from under his feet.

The conductor reached down
and opened a door in the stage.

"Oh!" he exclaimed.

"It's a bear!"

The conductor helped Paddington
climb onto the stage.
"Would you like to finish
the Surprise Symphony?" he asked.
He handed Paddington his baton.

Paddington waved the baton
in the air and then took his bow.
Everyone clapped and cheered.
It was a surprising end
to a most enjoyable day off!